Miss M K B E

THORNBURY
TO
BERKELEY
IN OLD PHOTOGRAPHS

THORNBURY TO BERKELEY

IN OLD PHOTOGRAPHS

COLLECTED BY

JOHN HUDSON

ALAN SUTTON
1987

Alan Sutton Publishing Limited
Brunswick Road · Gloucester

First published 1987

British Library Cataloguing in Publication Data

Thornbury to Berkeley in old photographs.
1. Thornbury (Avon)—History
2. Berkeley (Gloucestershire)—History
I. Hudson, John
942.3'91 DA690.T49

ISBN 0-86299-388-1

Typesetting and origination by
Alan Sutton Publishing Limited.
Printed in Great Britain
by WBC Print Limited · Bristol

CONTENTS

INTRODUCTION

When I was being interviewed for a newspaper article about this book I was asked whether an overall picture had emerged from its 200-plus images. After playing for time for a while – twenty years of posing journalistic questions have proved pathetically inadequate training for the occasional ten-minute stint of answering them – I drew some vague conclusion about the self-sufficiency and centuries-old stability of Victorian and Edwardian country life, with the blacksmith in his smithy, the grocer at his counter, the rich man in his castle and the poor man, as ever, doing as best he can.

Looking through the completed selection of photographs, I know what I meant when I said that, but perhaps it is all a two-dimensional illusion. Where would those self-sufficient shop-keepers have been without large imported consignments of Stephens' Ink, Virol, White Rose American Lamp Oils and Hudson's Soap? When social historians write of the upheavals of the farming crisis of the 1890s and the First World War, is it not both naïve and arrogant on our part to look at a picture of smiling estate tenants in the 1920s and conclude that the old order had changed not? The photographs will tell you time and again that the coming of the motor car has been the most potent agent of change in our towns and villages, but ask people who lived through the early years of this century and you will hear a different story: "It was the electric, you know".

So perhaps we should not read too many of our late-twentieth-century preconceptions into these images, but enjoy them for what they are – frozen split-seconds in the history of our communities conveying maybe a true picture, maybe a distorted one. I once worked with a photographer who had asked the Great Gigli to look as if he were singing; the Great Gigli, at the time, was mute with laryngitis. If cameras never lie, they are certainly capable of the occasional little fib.

They fib when they show Thornbury so little changed over a hundred years, the roofscapes of the High Street and Castle Street virtually untouched by time. What they do not show is the meadows and hedgerows of the Victorian days which are now Avon Way, Chiltern Park, Squires Leaze. Like "the electric", the spiritual change in a community is not a phenomenon to be captured on film; but because we are aware of it, there is added piquancy in scenes that have altered little in physical terms.

The growth of Berkeley has been markedly less dramatic, the influence of Bristol and the motorways almost minimal when compared with their impact on Thornbury. By current standards it remains a remote country town in a tucked-away pocket of England, so remote that the electricity generating board had no qualms about building Britain's first commercial nuclear power station on its doorstep.

You have only to peer over the Cotswold edge at Stinchcombe Hill or Coaley Peak to realise that the reactors at Berkeley and Oldbury are today's giants of the Vale, dwarfing the tallest church towers or castle turrets – but local people have accepted them as if they were simply haystacks in the yard, dwindling in their eyes with the passage of the seasons.

With few exceptions the pictures in this book cover the century from 1860 to 1960, with the middle fifty years of that timespan the dominant ones. Only in the past thirty years have changes been more than a natural, logical progression, a trimming of the sails to meet the local population's varying needs. In the 1920s, change was when one saddler took over the premises of an older partner; today it is a proposal for a 1,500-house estate convenient to the motorway junction.

In 1948 an old-timer was able to tell a Thornbury history group: "In what we call the shopping centre there has been very little change as regards businesses as long as I remember". At much the same time one of the contributors to this book recalls crossing Berkeley Market Place with her grandmother when a car happened by. "Good heavens," said the old lady, without irony. "It's busy round here today". The power station and castle, now a major tourist attraction, have wiped out at least that way of thinking.

A few words about my choice of photographs. I have tried hard for human interest, and fear I may occasionally have offended would-be contributors in doing so. Those glorious castles of Thornbury and Berkeley, the great houses, the churches, they have caused me more soul-searching than you would believe. What I have tried very hard to do is avoid good 1885 views of buildings that look like bad 1985 ones. Local architectural buffs might protest that this shot shows the west tower before the ivy was cut away, or that view was taken before 1936, when the eighth ball finial from the right fell off. Give me the little lads chasing the bus up the street, the long-nosed mummer, the chara trip to Weston. . .

The captions are as informative as space, initial information and the success of further research will allow. Having warned readers to take some of the pictures with a pinch of salt, I can only say that the facts and figures in my captions are accurate so far as I am aware; as for my opinions and speculations, if you have any salt left over from the pictures, you are welcome to reserve a grain or two for them.

Acknowledgements for the loan of pictures and information can be found on page 160, and I am grateful for the great kindness, help and co-operation I encountered – almost – every step of the way. I hope I offend no contributor if I make special mention here of the continuous support and encouragement of Mr Nick Large, Mr and Mrs Edwin Ford, Mrs Ann Riddiford, Mr and Mrs Henry Nurse, Mrs Valerie Vizard and the late and much missed Mr Ken Baily.

I make no excuse for my inclusion of the unveiling of the new Thornbury pump, but Ken's presence on that picture is a timely reminder that all the long-ago characters in this book in their odd coats and hats were just as much a force of nature, warm and vital, right sometimes, wrong sometimes, a funny old stick in some people's eyes and a dear friend in others'.

To borrow Dylan Thomas's already borrowed words, these pictures are not about the bricks and mortar of our communities, but for the love of Man and in praise of God (give or take one or two of His more boring looking houses); like Dylan, I'd be a damn' fool if they weren't.

John Hudson, Gloucestershire, 1987

SECTION ONE

Thornbury

ONE OF THE EARLIEST KNOWN PHOTOGRAPHS OF THORNBURY HIGH STREET, lacking many of the advertising signs familiar in photographs of the town in the Edwardian era. Fry the Saddler occupies the building long associated with Prewett's stationers, there is no evidence of Frank Symes's saddlery sign, which is so much a part of similar pictures from the early years of this century, and the old Market House has yet to be converted to Weatherhead's Drapery. On the opposite side of the road the swan is much in evidence on the hotel porch, and Gayner's draper's shop is also prominent, but the protruding sign that marked Councell's grocery, at the lower side of what is now St Mary's Way shopping arcade, has yet to appear. I have no firm evidence of what the flags signify; possibly Victoria's Golden Jubilee in 1887.

THE HIGH STREET EARLY IN 1906. Bristol Tramways sent their first double-decker bus out to Thornbury in February of that year, but the top deck was removed within weeks as overhanging trees endangered the passengers. The way the small boys are chasing the bus – one of twelve Thornycrofts bought by the tramways – suggests that it was still very much a novelty. By this time several familiar traders' signs have sprung up, but Weatherhead's have still not removed the first-floor roofing from around the Market House.

THERE WAS A PASSENGER LINE TO THORNBURY, ending at a station sited on the corner of Bristol Road and what is now Midland Way, from 1872 to 1942. This picture was taken almost exactly mid-way through this period.

THE TOP END OF THE HIGH STREET, reminding us that the mix of shops and residential properties is a long-established feature of this end of town. This picture was presumably taken on the roadsweeper's day off.

A SUPERB VIEW OF THE TOP END OF THE HIGH STREET, with the Exchange Hotel as a focal point. Just below are the Temperance Tea Rooms and Picture House opened on the site of the old Beaufort Hotel.

THE BUS, by now single-deck only, completes another run from Bristol. The shop to the left of the lamp-post belongs to Bernard Symes the tailor and breeches-maker, while the town had yet another saddler in Burchell and Embley.

THE FAMOUS HIGH STREET VIEW, *c.* 1909, showing Police Sergeant Vaughan, Dr Williams' Wolseley, the first car in Thornbury, and the sergeant's dog. He was called Patch, Sailor or Nipper, depending on who you talk to. Even the most notorious Thornburian rogue of the day could not have had so many aliases.

TWO VIEWS OF PREWETT'S STATIONERY SHOP. The premises are still run as a printer's and stationer's by the Horder family, who are related to the Prewetts. Heritage now occupy the premises to the left, and the Nell Gwyn Cafe those to the right.

THE 1920s – and the first inkling of the traffic congestion to come!

TWO PHOTOGRAPHS OF NO. 18 HIGH STREET, taken in 1916 and 1926. The top picture shows Mr Frank Symes, the saddler, who took on Mr Lawrence Roach of Falfield as his apprentice in 1916. Ten years later, with the boss retired, Mr Roach stands proudly outside his newly redecorated shop.

ST MARY'S WAY was the most revolutionary shopping development in Thornbury for centuries. It was opened by the Rural District Council chairman, Councillor Dr D.H. Fox just days before the old council was swept away by local government reform, on 25 March 1974. Now part of the larger St Mary Centre, the precinct has been modified extensively in recent years.

HIGH STREET TRADERS; the Golden Key, and below, the jeweller's shop run by Henry 'Clocky' Liddiatt, who was apprentice to a Clifton watchmaker in 1881. Note the 'nigger minstrel' clock, lower left, with the dial in his hat.

IN THE EARLY YEARS OF THIS CENTURY, bus crews looked as if they could fight a war for you. Fifty years on, *c*. 1960, the swan above the door presides over a rather different scene. John James, whose van can be seen right, had one of his television and electrical shops just above the Swan. He is now best known as a millionaire who gives fortunes away for charity.

ONE BUSINESS ALL OLD THORNBURIANS REMEMBER IS THOMPSON'S TEA ROOMS. It is there on the left, just above the Swan.

TWO VIEWS OF THE ORIGINAL PUMP ON THE PLAIN, the lower one considerably earlier than the upper. The figure in the centre of the group of three is holding a small penny-farthing bicycle.

THE PLAIN c. 1920. By this time the double-deck experiment has been abandoned completely, but it is still perfectly safe for buses to park in the centre of the carriageway.

GILBERT SYMES, ironmonger, who had his shop and foundry on the corner of The Plain next to the Royal George. The business was later taken over by his son Maurice, and both father and son can be seen in the family group on page 129.

1920s: GILBERT SYMES'S BUSINESS AND THE ROYAL GEORGE. The Pratt's Motor Spirit sign on the right is protruding from the shop on the corner of St John Street, which just happened to be run by someone called Symes. There was a fifth Symes shop in Thornbury, a confectioner's at the top end of the High Street close to what is now the MEB.

ST JOHN STREET looking from the Plain: the Symes shop is best remembered as a seed shop run by Rose, daughter of the confectioner Charlie. Trayhurn's the butchers were trading until comparatively recently.

DIGGING TRENCHES FOR WATER PIPES in St John Street, 1922. English's bread shop was one of a number of businesses on the street.

ST MARY STREET, only a few façades of which survive in the St Mary Centre shopping precinct. The property on the left, now the Compleat Cookshop, was the Church Institute, with a carved wooden porch dated 1679.

THE WIDE OPEN SWEEP OF THE PLAIN after the removal of the pump in 1924. See pages 152 to 154 for more on this famous Thornbury saga.

ST JOHN STREET, before it became detached from Pullins Green. The only significant change has taken place on the right, where several buildings, including the old Quaker Meeting House of 1676, were demolished in 1984 to make way for Quaker Court homes for the elderly.

PULLINS GREEN: the Manse, built in 1905, could not have been more than a couple of years old. Still to be built is the property to the left of it, now occupied by Adrian's Hairdressers. It is interesting to note that the building now used by the Hong Kong Fish Bar was a commercial property eighty years ago, selling wet fish. Another business on Pullins Green was a sweet shop run by Mrs Wall.

THE BERKELEY HUNT on The Plain in January, 1935.

AN EARLIER AND RATHER LESS CONGESTED VIEW OF THE PLAIN AND CASTLE STREET, pre 1924.

THE LOWER END OF CASTLE STREET, opposite the site of the new Northavon District Council offices. The business on the left is Salmon's the decorator.

A CLASSIC GROUPING: Thornbury's fourteenth-century church and Tudor castle.

Successive owners of Thornbury Castle have been rightly proud of its magnificent Tudor chimneys. They would not be standing today, however, if it had not been for Leonard Pitcher and his workmen, who restored them with great skill in 1904.

THE ORNATE AND HEAVILY ADORNED ENTRANCE TO THORNBURY CASTLE when it was the home of the Howard family early in this century. The castle remained in the family's hands until the mid 1960s when it became an exclusive restaurant. More recently it has widened its scope to become a country house hotel.

THE WAY SMALL MARKET TOWNS ALWAYS LOOK IN THE PICTURE BOOKS: Castle Street wends its way up to The Plain and the gentle hills beyond in this idyllic view from St Mary's Church tower.

SECTION TWO

Berkeley

A TRAP, A PRAM, AND ALL THE TIME IN THE WORLD to stand in the middle of the road: the High Street at the turn of the century.

PROGRESSING UP THE HIGH STREET, the mix is still one of private houses and business premises – as it is to this day. The White Lion later became an antiques shop and is now a private house.

THE MARKET PLACE, before the lower storey of the Town Hall was enclosed.

CONTEMPORARY VIEWS LOOKING EACH WAY FROM THE TOWN HALL in the early 1920s. Most photographs of charabancs we see nowadays are close-ups of parties aboard. The lower picture reminds us how odd and unwieldy they looked in the context of the street.

BUILDING THE POST OFFICE ON THE MARKET PLACE, 1908. Boots and shoes appear to be a preoccupation of the bill-posters.

THE OLD HOUSE on the corner of High Street and the Market Place is one of Berkeley's best-loved buildings, with the inscription RTE 1666 on its porch.

THE POST OFFICE of 1908; the building is now occupied by Richings the butchers.

STAGECOACHES were used to carry guests from the Berkeley Arms to the railway station at Berkeley Road until well into this century.

QUIET TIMES, BUSY TIMES: Edwardian Berkeley moved at a gentle pace, with little traffic to disturb pedestrians in the road. More animated was the scene in the Market Place in February 1939, when the traditional meet on the morning after the Berkeley Hunt Farmers' Ball attracted its usual heavy turn-out.

TRAFFIC CONGESTION at the Old House.

VIVIAN WARNER outside the High Street chemist's shop he took over on the death of his father George Oram – 'Joram' – in 1931. A picture of 'Joram' appears on page 116.

MACKINTOSH'S BUSINESS EMPIRE ON THE HIGH STREET; a pity about the discrepancy in the signs. The shop sold everything from drapery to hardware, but has long been converted back to private use. The old cottages on the left were demolished and replaced in 1907.

AN IMPROMPTU MARKET outside the Plough.

WHO SAID BERKELEY WAS A SLEEPY LITTLE PLACE? There's obviously something afoot here, with only the Bristol Mercury advertisement reminding us that it is not a scene from the old West.

ABOVE AND RIGHT: PROUD CANONBURY STREET TRADERS. Mr Miles the shoemaker, pictured in 1910, looks well equipped to carry out neatly executed repairs. Mr and Mrs Terrett are seen at their hardware shop in around 1930. The property is now a private house, but a painted advertisement for the Terretts' shop can still be seen on the wall.

H. TERRETT
LATE A. GARTON
Fluxite
DAY & MILLWARD LTD
WEIGHING
MACHINES
LEONARD THOMAS
& Cos
SPADES
FORKS SHOVELS
GARDEN TOOLS
NETTLEFOLDS
SCREWS
SIEMENS
ELECTRIC LAMPS
Reliance

A DUSTY SALTER STREET. Now the main road to the nuclear power station.

CONTEMPORARY VIEWS FROM THE YEARS BEFORE THE FIRST WORLD WAR: the hospital, a much-prized local facility, and Wallgaston, everything a gentleman's residence should be.

THOMAS ALPASS'S GENERAL STORES on the Market Place, a building now occupied by Fryer's newsagent's.

CANONBURY STREET with its stepped pavements.

Much has been done at the lower end of Canonbury Street in recent years to ensure that scenes like the one shown above are not repeated.

SUNLIGHT AND SHADOWS ON STATION ROAD.

DICKY PEARCE, reputed to have been the last private jester in England, died in drunken revelry in 1728. Jonathan Swift composed his epitaph, and his tomb has long been a point of interest in Berkeley churchyard.

IT IS A LONG TIME SINCE THE SEA MILLS AT BERKELEY WERE POWERED BY THE TIDES for Berkeley Pill has taken many a new twist since they were built. The mill building survives, however, and has acquired a number of thriving new businesses in recent years.

BERKELEY CASTLE early this century, with two views showing the ornate Chinese bell that once adorned its grounds.

THE LONG-DEMOLISHED OLD VICARAGE was the birthplace of Edward Jenner, the pioneer of vaccination. His later home was the Chantry, below, which has now been taken over as a conference centre and museum to commemorate his work.

THE PICTURESQUE JENNER'S HUT, in the grounds of the Chantry. It appears to be in sound order in this photograph from before the First World War, but it had fallen into a poor state of repair before being restored by admirers of the doctor's works in recent years.

A NEW SHAPE ON THE HORIZON: Berkeley Nuclear Power Station in 1958. To build the station the Conigre Pill was diverted, and it drained marshy land along its new course enabling farmer Hubert Spratt to cultivate it for the first time.

BERKELEY WAS BRITAIN'S FIRST COMMERCIAL NUCLEAR POWER STATION, and the press kept a close watch on its progress. This was how it looked after 25 months' work, in February 1959.

ALL SYSTEMS GO: The Duke of Edinburgh at the No. 1 reactor after formally opening the power station in April 1963.

SECTION THREE

Men at Work

MIGHTY MEAN HOMBRES: the workforce of Tucker Bros., builders, on site at the lower end of Thornbury High Street in 1901.

CULLIMORE'S WORKFORCE, 1899, shortly after fire had struck at the Thornbury sawmill.

SALMON FISHERMAN GEORGE HAINES (1869–1922), at Hayward's Rock, Clapton, near Berkeley. The large salmon baskets were kipes, bigger versions of the putchers which are stacked several rows deep.

MORE SALMON-FISHING ON THE SEVERN. The picture above is of Curty Weir, one of the fisheries lost in the building of Oldbury Nuclear Power Station.

LABOURERS WITH THEIR FARM MANAGER at Clapton Farm, near Berkeley, *c*. 1905.

THORNBURY FIRE BRIGADE before the First World War.

THIRSTY WORK: a cider sale at Rook Farm, Oldbury, in the 1950s.

OLIVER HIGGINS at his smithy in Crispin Lane, Thornbury, in 1929. On the right is his assistant Fred Pearce, who eventually took over from him.

NEALE'S GLEAMING ARRAY OF COACHES lines up for the camera in the 1950s.

WORKERS ON THE BERKELEY ESTATE around a hundred years ago. The men in the group above were all employed at the kennels.

THE OLD THORNBURY RURAL DISTRICT COUNCIL was proud of its steam rollers and traction engines. The depot was close to the railway station at the junction of Bristol Road and what is now Midland Way.

CHEERFUL ESTATE WORKERS at Tortworth, 1920s.

CHARLIE BENNETT AND JACK TYNDALL building the punt for Tortworth Lake in the 1920s. They did a good job. The boat is still floating.

JAMES BROWN with the Allen family's prize bull at Clapton Farm, near Berkeley, *c.* 1905.

WALTER FEAR, aged 12, with Fill Pail the shorthorn cow after she had won the champion's rosette at Berkeley Show in 1925. She was owned by Walter's father, Albert, of Yew Tree Farm, Upper Morton.

Until the new market was opened at Streamleaze in 1911, cattle sales were a regular feature – and hazard – of life in Thornbury. A view of the last street market appears on page 160.

SECTION FOUR

Happiest Days of their Life?

HEADMASTER CHARLES ROSS with a junior football team at Thornbury Grammar School, 1911. Mr Ross was head from 1907 to 1932, during which time the school expanded considerably.

THORNBURY GRAMMAR SCHOOL PUPILS process to the parish church in the early 1950s. At the head of the column is headmaster Mr S.J.V. Rouch, another formidable name in the school's history.

MAYDAY REVELS AT ROCKHAMPTON SCHOOL.

BOYS PLAYING AT HORSES AT ROCKHAMPTON SCHOOL *c.* 1900. There is a little more decorum about this formal study from the 1920s, below.

STANDARD SIX AT THORNBURY COUNCIL SCHOOL, 1906, with headmaster Mr Cresswell. The school later gave way to Leaze Primary.

ANOTHER STIFF AND STARCHY SCHOOL GROUP, this time, in spite of the photographer's caption, at Olveston.

MR ALGY SMITH AND MRS SMITH receive a retirement gift from Countess Ducie, with the seated fifth Earl and the Revd W. Peel looking on, in 1946. Mr Smith entered Tortworth School as a child of three, became a pupil teacher, and after a brief spell at college, returned as assistant master. Apart from a brief spell during the First World War he remained there for the rest of his career, and as he died shortly after his retirement as headmaster, he spent all but a handful of years of his life at Tortworth School.

TORTWORTH SCHOOL, *c.* 1926.

SEGREGATED SCHOOL PHOTOGRAPH, Berkeley Council School, 1920.

BOYS AT BERKELEY COUNCIL SCHOOL, 1907.

THE JUNIOR COUNCIL SCHOOL in Canonbury Street, Berkeley. This attractive building is now a restaurant.

SECTION FIVE

The Vale Villages

THE MEET OF THE BERKELEY HUNT to mark the twenty-first birthday of farmer Ben Neale's son Billy, the Gloucestershire cricketer, at Brookend Farm, near Berkeley.

THE STAR PUB AT HEATHFIELD, just north of Newport on the A38. The building is now a private house known as Star Inn Cottage.

NEWPORT CHAPEL and its neighbouring cottages have changed little externally over the years.

NEWPORT VILLAGE, before the A38 took its toll. On the right is the gateway to Newport Towers when it was still a private house, and beyond is the old Spread Eagle pub.

NEWPORT TOWERS, with its impressive bell tower, was a splendid Victorian house which later became a private hotel. It was destroyed by fire in 1947 and eventually replaced by the present motel.

THE FOX AT WOODFORD, on the eastern side of the A38. It is now an attractive family home, renamed Foxley House.

TEA ROOMS AND GARDENS were a feature of the main road through the Vale. The ones at Swanley, between Newport and Woodford, and on Stone Green are no more, but the Orange Umbrella still thrives at Falfield.

PICTURESQUE STONE POST OFFICE. The building still stands but the thatch has been replaced.

TWO MORE VIEWS OF STONE GREEN. Elms were a feature of the Berkeley Vale until Dutch Elm Disease struck in the 1970s.

PEACEFUL TIMES AT THE HUNTSMAN'S HOUSE AT FALFIELD. The cottage on the right of the lower photograph has given way to the pub car park.

A LESS PEACEFUL SCENE AT THE HUNTSMAN'S, in the 1950s.

LOOKING NORTH TOWARDS THE HUNTSMAN'S HOUSE AT FALFIELD. The gable end on the left is now part of the Falfield garage, but both the properties on the right have been demolished for road-widening.

THE ROUND HOUSE AT FALFIELD has had a chequered history, but it has recently been restored as a private house.

THE DEDICATION OF FALFIELD WAR MEMORIAL 1920.

MALVERN HOUSE, FALFIELD, was another substantial property to give way to road-widening. Seen here is Mrs Kate Tucker, whose husband John was a builder in Bristol, with her niece Miss Rose Stevens.

FALFIELD LOOKING NORTH, with Sundayshill Lane on the left. On the right is Malvern House.

FALFIELD showing yet more properties that fell prey to road-widening, a row of cottages attached to the Post Office.

VINE COTTAGE, ROCKHAMPTON, showing the Gothic architecture typical of Berkeley country.

AN IDYLLIC SCENE outside Rockhampton Church in 1910.

THE OLD POST OFFICE AT ROCKHAMPTON, now Springfield, in around 1910. In the distance, at the top of the road, can be seen an ancient white boundary stone which was rediscovered during road works in recent years and resited as near as possible to its original spot.

FÊTE to raise funds for Rockhampton church restoration, *c.* 1958.

MRS GOUGH AND MRS HART at Rockhampton Church, 1910.

THE BERKELEY HOUNDS at Rockhampton Green, watched by an interested toddler.

THE BERKELEY HUNT AT TORTWORTH GREEN. The house in the picture is the orphanage founded by the third Countess Ducie, which was closed in the early 1900s. The building, however, survives.

TORTWORTH COURT when it was still the Ducies' home. Built by the second Earl in the 1850s, it was in institutional hands from the Second World War until 1987, when it was sold by the prison department.

A MEET OF THE BERKELEY HUNT at the Rose at Huntingford in 1948. Note the spectators' bicycles strewn along the hedgerow.

ROSE INN

ANOTHER VIEW OF TORTWORTH COURT at its well-manicured finest.

OLD COTTAGES AT HAM. The thatched properties have now been demolished.

WHITE ELM COTTAGE AT CLAPTON, near Berkeley, demolished in the 1940s. The tree in its garden was regarded by locals as a weather indicator. If the leaves looked white in the spring it would be a dry summer.

OLD BLUE GATES FARMHOUSE AT CLAPTON, Berkeley, *c.* 1880. The couple in the light carriage are Charles and Stella Ford, tenant farmers on the Berkeley Estate. The building is still standing, but in a desperate state of repair.

AN ARTISTIC POSE ON THE RIVER BANK AT SHEPPERDINE, around 1900. The photographer was almost certainly a daughter of William Richmond, Rector of Rockhampton from 1889 to 1911; the model could well have been another of his daughters.

THE WINDBOUND PUB AT SHEPPERDINE was originally the New Inn, but it has been trading under its sailors' nickname for many years, as this postcard shows. The mock Tudor wing on the left has been replaced by a large modern extension.

THE SWAN AT TYTHERINGTON, receiving bread supplies from Trayhurn's delivery van.

THE SHIP AT ALVESTON is a famous coaching inn, but it looks disappointingly suburban in this photograph from around 1905.

ST ARILDA'S CHURCH AT OLDBURY before its restoration in 1885.

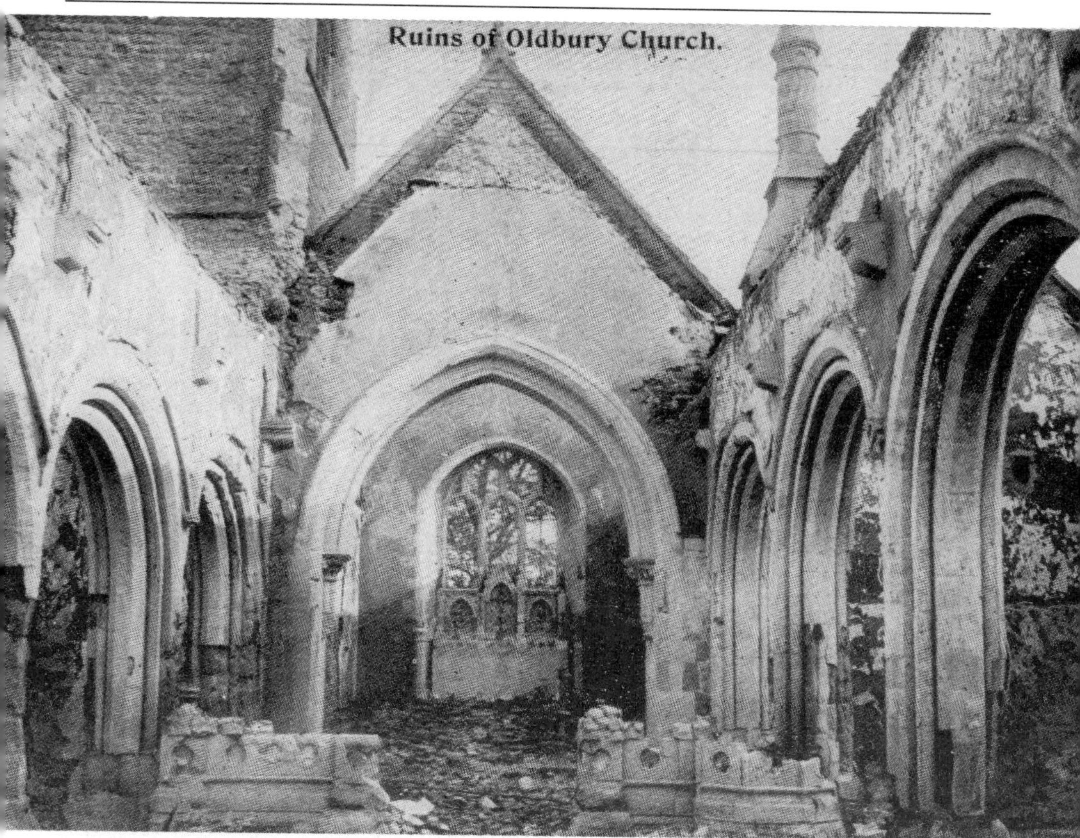

THE 1885 RESTORATION lasted only twelve years before Oldbury Church was devastated by fire after an accident with an oil appliance. An appeal was launched, and by 1899 the church had been rebuilt.

ANOTHER SCENE OF DEVASTATION at Oldbury Church, 1897.

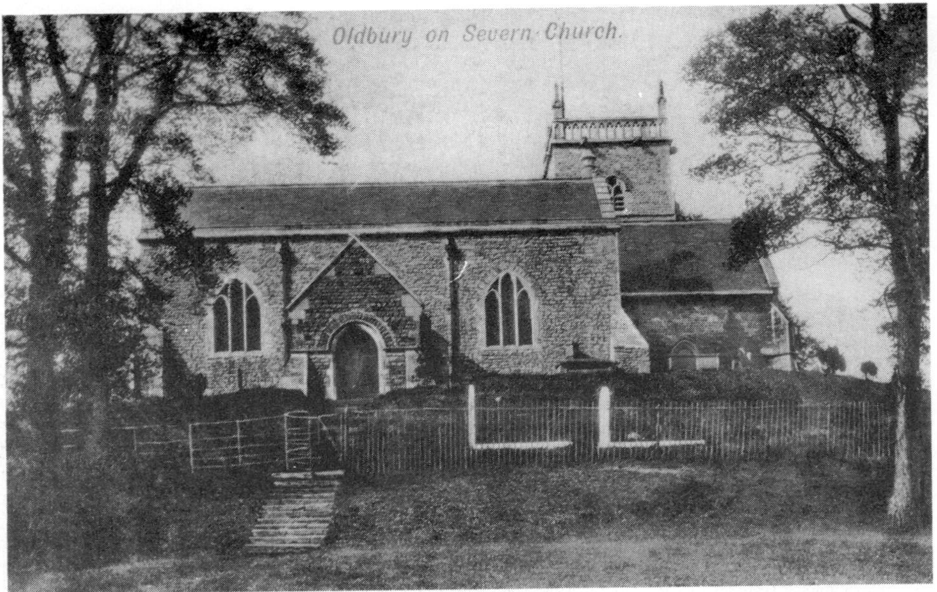

THE CHURCH AFTER THE RESTORATION. The architect was Waller, who did much Gothic Revival work in Gloucestershire.

OLDBURY VILLAGE, with the Ship Inn as a focal point.

OLDBURY PILL in around 1920, when it was still a port for small coal boats from South Wales.

A YEAR'S PROGRESS AT OLDBURY NUCLEAR POWER STATION, from early 1963, above, to January 1964, below. The station was opened by the then Technology Minister, Mr Anthony Wedgwood Benn, in June, 1969.

SECTION SIX

Meet the Folks

TORTWORTH ESTATE WORKERS c.1895, with the long-serving third Earl. In spite of his distinguished white beard, he lived another quarter-century after this picture was taken, holding office from 1853 to 1921.

MAURICE NEALE, of the sporting Berkeley Vale family, in the colours of Bristol Rugby Club. Born and bred at Brookend Farm, he played for Bristol, Blackheath and the Barbarians, and captained England in South Africa in 1910.

JAMES ELEY (1805–1861), Berkeley saddler.

GEORGE MILLS, thatcher of White Elm cottage, Clapton, *c.* 1859.

BERKELEY ESTATE TENANT FARMERS, rent audit day, the Berkeley Arms Hotel, 1920s.

AESTHETIC CYCLIST, Berkeley Church, *c.* 1890.

GEORGE ORAM 'JORAM' WARNER, Berkeley Chemist and mainstay of the Plymouth Brethren at Pittbrook. His bicycle is a Pedersen, made in Dursley in the early years of this century by a Danish engineer.

BERKELEY BUTCHER JOE KING with sturgeon, July 1953. It was caught by Harry Bennett in one of the battery of putchers – 'fixed engines' – along the Severn. It is customary for the lord of the manor of Berkeley to offer the Royal fish to the reigning monarch, and our young queen was happy to accept the gift. Harry Bennett tells an hilarious tale about the journey from Berkeley to the Palace. A high spot was when the truck broke down on the Tetbury–Cirencester road, the fish in its white wrappings was laid on the grass verge, and passengers in passing cars raised their hats in respect of what they took to be the victim of a fatal road accident.

BERKELEY HOME GUARD, Chantry garden, 1944.

REGULARS AT THE PLUME OF FEATHERS, Brookend, nr. Berkeley, 1920. The pub is now a private house owned by Mr Aubrey Neale of the sporting Vale family.

BERKELEY BANDSMEN, date unknown.

THORNBURY BAPTIST PRIZE BAND, *c.* 1910.

THE OPENING OF THE MUNDY PLAYING FIELDS, Thornbury, 1937. General and Mrs Mundy lived at Thornbury House, and the land was donated to the town after her husband's death by Mrs Violet Mundy. The picture shows parish council chairman Mr Charlie Pitcher receiving the deeds. Doctor E.M. Grace is on the left, and centre is Lord Bledisloe of Lydney Park.

NOT QUITE WHAT IT SEEMS: an 'old-style' cricket match played in comparatively recent times, though under all those whiskers it is hard to say by whom and when.

Being on the main route between John O'Groats and Land's End, the A38 has seen some colourful characters over the years. Above is Doctor Barbara Moore, an eccentric who caught Britain's imagination with her fitness fanaticism in 1960. Below, the cricketer Ian Botham looks like some latter-day pied piper as he leaves Newport Towers for another leg of his outstandingly successful walk for leukaemia funds in 1985.

SERGEANT S. SYMES of Thornbury seated centre, with Royal Engineers colleagues and servants Fa Yheun, Fa Gui and Ah Fat, *c.* 1890. Sergeant Symes, related to blacksmith Gilbert, fought in Egypt and Sudan in the 1880s and was a Company Sergeant Major by the time the Boer War came around.

GEORGE HAINES, Private in the Fourth Hussars in India, with his mother Hannah and sister Selina in around 1895. The family lived at Shepperdine, but the picture was taken in a Castle Street, Thornbury, studio.

FARMER'S BOYS. Brothers Ben and Hastings Neale of Brookend Farm.

CHEEKY CHAPPIE: Frank Child of Green Farm, Rockhampton, *c.* 1900.

A LATER PICTURE OF FRANK CHILD, beating carpets in the Rectory gardens. The goal posts in the background were for the ladies' hockey team that flourished at Rockhampton in the early years of this century.

ROCKHAMPTON RECTORS AND THEIR FAMILIES: Above, the Revd. Osmond Currie Huntley, 1886–1889; and below, the Revd. William Richmond, 1880–1911.

THORNBURY IRONMONGER AND BLACKSMITH GILBERT SYMES AND FAMILY. The elder boy, Maurice, went on to take over the business.

MATTHEW AND MARY FORD, who married in 1850, with what appears to be rather more daughters than a farmer would wish to have. The family lived at Court Farm, Rockhampton.

BERKELEY FOOTBALLERS, *c*.1920.

THE GRACE FAMILY CRICKET TEAM pictured in about 1867 at Knowle Park, Almondsbury. A young W.G. is on the extreme left. Centre in the middle row is Dr E.M., father of the Thornbury GP.

THORNBURY CRICKET CLUB VS. THE SHIP HOTEL, August 1956. The Ship won by seven wickets.

BERKELEY LAWN TENNIS CLUB, pre 1914.

FARMER JOHN NEALE of Brookend with his wife, eleven children, livestock and guns.

FALFIELD VILLAGERS *c.* 1935.

INAUGURATION OF FALFIELD CRICKET PAVILION, Eastwood Park, 1949.

FALFIELD FOOTBALL CLUB, 1931–32. With their red and green strip they were known as the Parrots in the days long before beaten footballers felt as sick as that particular bird.

HALMORE FOOTBALL TEAM on Norman Neale's old Chevrolet truck. He would take cattle to market in it in the morning, sluice it down and carry the lads to their away matches in the afternoon.

VIC JONES with 7lb. salmon lave-netting at Shepperdine, August 1971.

Captain George Nicholls and daughters, *c.* 1890. He was a publican, trow-owner and coal merchant in and around Berkeley.

HENRY AND JULIA RICE and their family at Avening Green, Tortworth, *c.* 1914. Henry was a labourer who worked on both farms and the railway.

THE REVD MR CORNWALL and the Vicar's Bible Class, Thornbury, pre-First World War.

SECTION SEVEN

High Days and Holidays

THE COMMEMORATION OF QUEEN VICTORIA'S DIAMOND JUBILEE, The Plain, Thornbury, 28 June, 1897. It seems rather a sparse turnout on a sunless day, with scarcely a flag to be seen and the pump without any adornments.

THORNBURY PARISH COUNCIL CHAIRMAN W.D. CANNING announcing the Relief of Mafeking, 1900.

PROCLAIMING THE NEW KING, GEORGE V, at the court house, Thornbury, May 1910.

MILITARY HEROES about whom no-one seems to recall very much today: the Old Down Troop cutting a dash in Thornbury, above and right.

RETURN OF OLDOWN TROOP.
F.C.P

WARTIME PATRIOTISM: guarding the flag on Empire Day, 1915.

THE FUNERAL PROCESSION OF PRIVATE HECTOR PENDUCK of the Royal Army Medical Corps enters Thornbury churchyard, February 1915.

THE FIRST WORLD WAR HAD A HAPPIER OUTCOME FOR ARTHUR HILL, though he was badly wounded in action. The picture shows his marriage to Florence Smart in the spring of 1919, taken in the garden of her parents' home at Berkeley Road.

ABOVE AND RIGHT, TWO VIEWS OF THE PLAIN, Thornbury, on the declaration of peace in 1918. The pump is a mass of flags and foliage, with the Stars and Stripes prominent among the Union Jacks.

THE PROCLAMATION OF PEACE, The Plain, Thornbury, 1918.

A BERKELEY PROCESSION *c.* 1910. A banner proclaiming 'Votes For Women' gives a clue to the date.

LITTLETON PILL was a magnet for people from miles around in January 1885 when a huge whale was stranded in its narrow waters. Sixty-eight feet long, it pulled in the crowds for a fortnight before its stench prompted locals to have it towed away down to Avonmouth to be converted into fish manure. The area is still known as Whale Wharf, and copies of this picture can be seen all over the district.

LITTLE RED RIDING HOOD and her friends raised funds for Rockhampton Band of Hope in 1910.

BIG SMILES AND BLACK LOOKS: The Thornbury Methodist Minstrels on their carnival float, mid 1930s.

THORNBURY MUMMING GROUP in the early years of this century. There have been various moves to revive the tradition over the years.

ANOTHER RICH CHAPTER IN THORNBURY'S FOLK HISTORY: the removal of the pump from the Plain by officialdom in the autumn of 1924, and the persistent efforts of a group of locals to restore it. The signpost shown right was put up by wags, no doubt in an effort to prove that there was no substitute for the original wrought iron structure, but the battle was lost until a replica took its place on the Plain in 1984.

To BRISTOL
To GLOUCESTER

THE RETURN OF THE PUMP – sixty years on. Thornbury's mayor, Councillor Francis Hopkins, performs the opening ceremony watched by Concern for Thornbury chairman Mr Ken Baily, a former Sunday newspaper showbiz correspondent who threw himself wholeheartedly into the life of the town until his death in 1987.

COACH PARTY from Thornbury to Berkeley, September 1900.

ON THE CHARA TO WESTON: an outing from Mount Pleasant Chapel, Falfield, in 1925, and below, a men's group from Berkeley at around the same time.

FLOWER SHOW PROCESSION, Thornbury High Street, 1909.

BERKELEY HOME GUARD parading through the Market Place, 1945.

ABOVE AND LOWER LEFT, THE CHIEF SCOUT, LORD ROWALLAN, takes the salute in Berkeley Market Place, *c.* 1950.

THE LAST STREET MARKET IN THORNBURY, 1911.

ACKNOWLEDGEMENTS

Thanks for the loan of pictures, background information or other help are due to:

The late Mr Ken Baily • Mr Bill Bawden • Mr John Blake • Mrs M. Blenkinsopp
Mrs M. Browning • Mrs Margaret Burgess • Mr Stephen Budd
Mrs Jacqueline Clark • Mr John Cope MP • Mr Charles Eardley-Wilmot
Mr D. Emes • Mr Edwin and • Mrs Carole Ford • Canon Eric Gethyn-Jones
Mrs S. Gordon • Mr Spencer Green • Mr H. Greenway • Mr Robert Haines
the Misses Sarah and Nancy Hayes • Miss J. Higgins • Mr D. Horder
Miss Claire Hudson • Mr N.F. Large • Mr Mervyn Malpass • the late Mr I. Mills
Mr R. Mills • Mr Aubrey Neale • Mrs M. Nottingham • Mr and Mrs Henry Nurse
Mrs Doreen Partridge • the late Mrs Rose Perkins • Miss Helen Pitcher
Mrs Vivien Rees • Mrs Mary Riddle • Mrs Ann Riddiford • Mr W.L. Roach
Mrs N. Robinson • the Screen Family • Mr Ken Sheppard • Mrs Ethel Thomas
Thornbury Cricket Club • Mr Michael J. Tozer • the late Mr R. Tucker
Mrs Valerie Vizard • the late Miss A. Worsley.